U.S. DEPARTMENT OF LABOR   Occupational Safety and Health Administration

DIRECTIVE NUMBER: 11-04 (FAP 01)   **EFFECTIVE DATE:** December 23, 2011
SUBJECT: Federal Agency Targeting Inspection Program 2012 (FEDTARG12)

ABSTRACT

Purpose: The Occupational Safety and Health Administration (OSHA) *Federal Agency Targeting Inspection Program* (FEDTARG) is a fiscal year (FY) based, programmed inspection program focusing on specific federal agency service/operating locations reporting high numbers of lost time cases. In addition, the directive raises Regional awareness about the use of federal agency alternate and supplementary standards in developing local emphasis programs. This directive implements FEDTARG for FY 2012.

Scope: OSHA-wide.

References: Occupational Safety and Health Act of 1970, Section 19; Executive Order 12196, February 26, 1980; 29 CFR Part 1952, Approved State Plans for Enforcement of State Standards; 29 CFR Part 1960, Basic Program Elements for Federal Employee Occupational Safety and Health Programs and Related Matters; OSHA Instruction ADM 03-01-005, OSHA Compliance Records, August 3, 1998; OSHA Instruction CPL 02-00-025, Scheduling System for Programmed Inspections, January 4, 1995; OSHA Instruction CPL 02-00-135, Recordkeeping Policies and Procedures Manual, December 30, 2004; OSHA Instruction CPL 02-00-150, Field Operations Manual, April 22, 2011; OSHA Instruction CPL 02-02-072, Rules of Agency Practice and Procedure Concerning OSHA Access to Employee Medical Records for Policy Regarding Review of Medical and Exposure Records, August 22, 2007;OSHA Instruction CSP 03-01-003, Voluntary Protection Programs (VPP): Policies and Procedures Manual, April 18, 2008; OSHA Instruction CSP 03-02-002, OSHA Strategic Partnership Program for Worker Safety and Health, February 10, 2005; and OSHA Instruction FAP 01-00-003, Federal Agency Safety and Health Programs, May 17, 1996.

Cancellations: This directive cancels OSHA Notice 10-08 (FAP 01), Federal Agency Targeting Inspection Program (FEDTARG11), dated November 15, 2010; and OSHA Instruction FAP 01-00-005, FAA Airport Traffic Control Tower Monitoring Program (AIRTRAF), dated June 22, 2009.

Expiration Date: This directive expires on September 30, 2012, unless replaced earlier by a new directive. Upon the expiration or replacement of this directive, inspection cycles already underway must be completed as provided for in this directive.

State Plan Impact: This directive applies solely to federal agency service/operating locations. It does not impact State Plan programs.

Action Offices: National, Regional, and Area Offices.

Originating Office: Directorate of Enforcement Programs.

Contact: Directorate of Enforcement Programs
Office of Federal Agency Programs (OFAP)
200 Constitution Avenue, NW, N-3622
Washington, D.C. 20210

Telephone: (202) 693-2122
Facsimile: (202) 693-1685

By and Under the Authority of

David Michaels, PhD, MPH
Assistant Secretary

Executive Summary

This directive describes the Occupational Safety and Health Administration (OSHA) *Federal Agency Targeting Inspection Program* (FEDTARG) for fiscal year (FY) 2012. It defines key terms, describes the development process of FEDTARG inspection lists, outlines scheduling and inspection procedures for federal establishments, and provides information on inspection coding within the Integrated Management Information System (IMIS), and the OSHA Information System (OIS). In addition, the directive raises Regional awareness about the use of federal agency alternate and supplementary standards in developing local emphasis programs. The directive includes two appendices. Appendix A describes the handling of federal establishment participation in the Voluntary Protection Programs and the OSHA Strategic Partnership Program (OSPP), and explains IMIS/ OIS coding terminology. Appendix B provides a reference for the abbreviations, acronyms and symbols used in this directive.

Significant Changes for FEDTARG 2012

- Reorganized the directive to more closely follow the inspection process established in the OSHA Field Operations Manual.
- Added the provision for reviewing applicable federal agency alternate and supplementary standards as part of the preparatory process for an inspection.
- Added the provision for Regions to develop their own special emphasis programs for federal agencies having alternate and/or supplementary standards.
- Added the provision for an OSHA area office to request that the federal establishment office processing a special personal security clearance maintain the "unannounced" status of the upcoming inspection, whenever possible.
- Added a reference to the general duty requirements for federal agencies.
- Clarified the process of creating a secondary inspection list.
- Clarified the Area Director's decision-making process to conduct additional inspections at establishments with multiple service/operations and/or office-only operating locations.
- Defined the terms "alternate standard" and "supplementary standard."
- Deleted the need to provide the random number originally assigned to a federal establishment when the Region is requesting a secondary inspection list.
- Provided examples of circumstances when a Regional Administrator may request approval from the Assistant Secretary of Labor for OSHA to delete establishments from an inspection list.

Table of Contents

I. Purpose. The Occupational Safety and Health Administration (OSHA) Federal Agency *Targeting Inspection Program* (FEDTARG) is a fiscal year (FY) based, programmed inspection program focusing on specific federal agency service/operating locations reporting a high number of lost time cases (LTCs) through the U.S Department of Labor - Office of Workers' Compensation Programs (OWCP). In addition, the directive raises Regional awareness about the use of federal agency alternate and supplementary standards in developing local emphasis programs. This directive implements FEDTARG for FY 2012.

II. Scope. This directive applies OSHA-wide.

III. References.

   A. Title 29 United States Code 651, Occupational Safety and Health Act of 1970, Section 19, *Federal Agency Safety Programs and Responsibilities.*

   B. Executive Order 12196, *Occupational Safety and Health Programs for Federal Employees.* February 26, 1980.

   C. 29 CFR Part 1904, *Recording and Reporting Occupational Injuries and Illnesses,* 66 FR 5916-6135, January 19, 2001, and as amended.

   D. 29 CFR Part 1952, *Approved State Plans for Enforcement of State Standards,*

   E. 29 CFR Part 1960, *Basic Program Elements for Federal Employee Occupational Safety and Health Programs and Related Matters,* October 21, 1980, and as amended.

   F. 29 CFR Part 1960, Subpart I, *Recordkeeping and Reporting Requirements*; 69 FR 68793-68805, November 26, 2004.

   G. Directives.

   • ADM 03-01-005, OSHA Compliance Records, OSHA Instruction, August 3, 1998.

   • CPL 02-00-025, Scheduling System for Programmed Inspections, OSHA Instruction, January 4, 1995.

   • CPL 02-00-135, Recordkeeping Policies and Procedures Manual, OSHA Instruction, December 30, 2004.

- <u>CPL 02-00-150</u>, Field Operations Manual (FOM), April 22, 2011.

- <u>CPL 02-02-072</u>, Rules of Agency Practice and Procedure Concerning OSHA Access to Employee Medical Records for Policy Regarding Review of Medical and Exposure Records, OSHA Instruction, August 22, 2007.

- <u>CSP 03-01-003</u>, Voluntary Protection Programs (VPP): Policies and Procedures Manual, OSHA Instruction, April 18, 2008.

- <u>CSP 03-02-002</u>, OSHA Strategic Partnership Program for Worker Safety and Health, OSHA Instruction, February 10, 2005.

- <u>FAP 01-00-003</u>, Federal Agency Safety and Health Programs, OSHA Instruction, May 17, 1996.

IV.   <u>Cancellations</u>. This directive cancels OSHA Notice 10-08 (FAP 01), Federal Agency Targeting Inspection Program (FEDTARG11), dated November 15, 2010; and OSHA Instruction FAP 01-00-005, FAA Airport Traffic Control Tower Monitoring Program (AIRTRAF), dated June 22, 2009.

V.   <u>Expiration Date</u>. This directive expires on September 30, 2012, unless replaced earlier by a new directive. Upon the expiration or replacement of this directive, inspection cycles already underway must be completed, as provided for in this directive.

VI.   <u>Federal Program Change</u>. This directive applies solely to the inspection of federal establishments' service/operating locations. It does not impact State Plan programs.

VII.   <u>Background</u>.

<u>Executive Order 12196</u>, *Occupational Safety and Health Programs for Federal Employees*, paragraph 1-401(i) requires Federal OSHA to:

> Conduct unannounced inspections of agency workplaces when the Secretary determines necessary if an agency does not have occupational safety and health <u>committees</u>; or in response to <u>reports</u> of unsafe or unhealthful working conditions, upon request of occupational safety and health committees under Section 1-3; or, in the case of a report of an imminent danger, when such a committee has not responded to an employee who has alleged to it that the agency has not adequately responded to a report as required in 1-201(h). When the Secretary or his designee performs an inspection and discovers unsafe or unhealthy conditions, a violation of any provisions of this order, or any safety or health standards adopted by an agency pursuant to this order, or any program element approved by the Secretary, he shall promptly issue a report to the head of the agency and to the appropriate

occupational safety and health committee, if any. The report shall describe the nature of the findings and may make recommendations for correcting the violation.

VIII.   <u>Significant Changes</u>. The revised directive has been reorganized to more closely follow the inspection process established in the OSHA Field Operations Manual. It also:

- Adds the provision for reviewing applicable federal agency alternate and supplementary standards as part of the inspection preparatory process.
- Adds the provision for Regions to develop their own special emphasis programs for federal agencies having alternate and/or supplementary standards.
- Adds the provision for an OSHA area office to request that the federal establishment office processing a special personal security clearance maintain the "unannounced" status of the upcoming inspection, whenever possible.
- Adds a reference to the general duty requirements for federal agencies at 29 CFR 1960.8, *Agency responsibilities.*
- Clarifies the process of creating a secondary inspection list.
- Clarifies the Area Director's decision-making process to conduct additional inspections at establishments with multiple service/operations and/or office-only operating locations.
- Defines the terms "alternate standard" and "supplementary standard."
- Deletes the need to provide the random number originally assigned to a federal establishment when the Region is requesting a secondary inspection list.
- Provides examples of circumstances when a Regional Administrator may request approval from the Assistant Secretary of Labor for OSHA to delete establishments from an inspection list.

IX.   <u>Action Required</u>.

A.   <u>Responsible Office</u>. The Directorate of Enforcement Programs (DEP), through the Office of Federal Agency Programs (OFAP), coordinates the development of FEDTARG, manages the overall Program, and advises the Assistant Secretary of Labor for OSHA concerning FEDTARG issues.

B.   <u>Action Offices</u>. All National Office Directorates and Offices, Regional Offices, and Area Offices involved in the development, approval, and implementation of this inspection targeting program must adhere to this directive.

C.   <u>Information Offices</u>. The OSHA Training Institute, Voluntary Protection Programs Managers and Coordinators, OSHA Strategic Partnership Program Coordinators, Compliance Assistance Coordinators, Compliance Assistance Specialists, Federal Agency Program Officers, and Regional Enhanced

Enforcement Program Coordinators must be aware of this inspection targeting program.

X.   Definitions.

A.   *Alternate Standard.* Consistent with the *Field Operations Manual* (FOM), Chapter 13, paragraph III.F., Alternate and Supplementary Standards, the term "alternate standard" refers to the federal agency equivalent of a private sector variance from OSHA standards. A current listing of approved alternate standards is provided in paragraph XIV. B., *Use of Alternate, Supplementary Standards,* in this directive; and on the OFAP web page.

B.   *Certified Safety and Health Committee (CSHC).* For the purposes of this directive, the term "CSHC" refers to a federal agency safety and health committee meeting the provisions of section 1-3 of *Executive Order 12196,* and of *29 CFR Part 1960,* Subpart F, as listed and attested to by the head of each agency, in writing to the Secretary of Labor.

Currently, the following federal agencies have CSHCs: Central Intelligence Agency, Tennessee Valley Authority, U.S. Department of Labor, U.S. General Services Administration, U.S. International Trade Commission, and U.S. Securities and Exchange Commission.

C.   *Comprehensive Inspection.* Consistent with the *Field Operations Manual* (FOM), Chapter 3, paragraph III.A., Comprehensive, the term "comprehensive inspection" refers to a:

> [S]ubstantially complete inspection of the potentially high hazard areas of an establishment. An inspection may be deemed comprehensive even though, as a result of the exercise of professional judgment, not all potentially hazardous conditions, operations, and practices within those areas are inspected.

D.   *Deferral.* For purposes of this directive, the term "deferral" refers to a delay of an inspection of a specific federal agency's service/operating location due to its participation in or application to Voluntary Protection Programs. A deferred federal establishment will be inspected at the end of the agency's deferral period. Further guidance may be found in CPL 02-00-150, Chapter 2, VI.H. - Inspection Scheduling and Interface with Cooperative Program Participants, and Chapter 3, V.D. - Review of Voluntary Compliance Programs; and CSP 03-01-003, Chapter II, VII.A. – Inspection Deferrals.

E.   *Establishment*. Consistent with 29 CFR 1960.2(h), Definitions, and as applied to federal agencies, the term "establishment" refers to a:

> [S]ingle physical location where business is conducted or where services or operations are performed. Where distinctly separate activities are performed at a single physical location, each activity will be treated as a separate establishment and inspection. Typically, an establishment refers to a federal agency's field activity, regional office, area office, installation, or facility.

F.   *Federal Agency*. For the purposes of this directive, the term "federal agency" refers to an Executive Department, as identified in *U.S. Code Title 5, Part 1, Chapter 1, §101*, or any employing unit, or authority of the Executive Branch of the Government. For the purposes of this directive, it does not include the United States Postal Service.

G.   *Lost Time Case* (LTC). For purposes of this directive, the term "LTC" is defined as a federal employee's compensation case reported to the Office of Workers' Compensation Programs wherein the federal employee loses time from work beyond the date of the injury.

H.   *Office of Workers' Compensation Programs* (OWCP) *Data*. The U.S. Department of Labor - OWCP administers the Federal Employees' Compensation Program, as defined under the Federal Employees' Compensation Act. OWCP administers four (4) major disability compensation programs that provide wage replacement benefits, medical treatment, vocational rehabilitation, and other benefits to certain workers or their dependents who experience work-related injury or occupational disease. The data generated from the previous FY through the OWCP claims process, specifically the number of lost time cases experienced by federal agencies, is used to generate the FEDTARG inspection lists (primary and secondary).

I.   *Partial Inspection*. Consistent with the *Field Operations Manual* (FOM), Chapter 3, paragraph III.B. Partial, the term "partial inspection" refers to an inspection "…whose focus is limited to certain potentially hazardous areas, operations, conditions, or practices at the establishment." The compliance safety and health officer (CSHO), in consultation with the Area Director (AD), must use professional judgment to determine the necessity for expanding the inspection's scope. Minimally, this decision should be based on information gathered during the records/program review and walkaround inspection. CSP 03-02-002, paragraph XIV.B.4. refers to this type of inspection as a *programmed inspection with a limited scope* for OSHA Strategic Partnership Program for Worker Safety and Health participants.

J.   *Supplementary Standard.* Consistent with the *Field Operations Manual* (FOM), Chapter 13, paragraph III.F., Alternate and Supplementary Standards, the term "supplementary standard" refers to an occupational safety and health standard developed and implemented by a federal agency in accordance with the process described in 29 CFR 1960.18. A federal agency must implement a supplementary standard when no OSHA standard is applicable to a given workplace hazard. A current listing of approved supplementary standards is provided in paragraph XIV. B., *Use of Alternate, Supplementary Standards,* in this directive and on the OFAP web page.

XI.   Federal Establishment-Specific Targeting Program Planning

A.   General. FEDTARG is directed toward federal agency establishments experiencing high numbers of lost time cases. OFAP obtains establishment-specific lost time claims data from OWCP. This data is used to develop the primary and, if requested, secondary inspection lists. The inspection lists include the agency name, number of claims and fatalities, and limited establishment location information.

B.   Completion of Inspection Lists. Once opened, all establishments on an inspection list (primary or secondary) must be inspected, unless deferred or deleted from inspection by the Regional Administrator (RA) or AD, in accordance with the *Field Operations Manual* (FOM), and paragraph XII.D. *FEDTARG Inspection Deferrals: Interface with Cooperative Program Participants,* or paragraph XII.E., *FEDTARG Inspection Deletions,* of this directive.

C.   Types of FEDTARG Inspection Lists.

1.   Primary Inspection List.

a.   OFAP develops a primary inspection list (also referred to as an "inspection cycle" in this directive) based on the OWCP data list (see paragraph X.H., *Office of Workers' Compensation Programs Data,* in this directive). Federal establishments are randomly selected from the OWCP data list; then, partitioned by relevant OSHA Region.

b.   Each Regional primary inspection list includes: 100% of the establishments within the Region's jurisdiction reporting 100 or more LTCs, 50% of the establishments reporting 50 to 99 LTCs, and 10% of the establishments reporting 20 to 49 LTCs.

c. This targeting process assumes that an adequate number of establishments are available for inclusion on the primary inspection list.

d. OFAP maintains the original randomized OWCP data list of remaining establishments from the current FEDTARG in case the Regional federal agency program officer (FAPO) requests secondary inspection lists.

2. Secondary Inspection List.

a. The National Office (NO) recognizes that resources available for conducting FEDTARG inspections will vary widely among the Regional (RO) and Area Offices (AO). Those offices having the resources to conduct additional FEDTARG inspections than provided for by their primary inspection lists may request secondary inspection lists.

b. Upon request, OFAP will provide the FAPO with a secondary inspection list of federal establishments that fall within the scope of FEDTARG and Regional jurisdiction. From this list, the FAPO will develop separate lists for the requesting AOs, as necessary.

c. The secondary inspection list will be comprised of the number of establishments requested by the RO, to include 60% of the establishments reporting 50 to 99 LTCs, and 40% of those reporting 20 to 49 LTCs. If less than the requested number of establishments from the OWCP list remain, the secondary list will be comprised of all remaining establishments.

XII. <u>FEDTARG Planning and Scheduling</u>.

A. <u>General</u>. The NO will provide each OSHA Region with a list of establishments within its coverage area meeting the criteria for the primary inspection list (see paragraph XI.C.1., *Primary Inspection List*, in this directive). OFAP will handle requests for a secondary inspection in accordance with paragraph XI.C.2., *Secondary Inspection List*, in this directive.

1. In instances when the exact physical address of an establishment's service/operating location is uncertain, the AO should attempt to identify the exact location of the establishment's service/operating location to be inspected.

2.   An AO must complete the inspection of the establishments on the primary inspection list prior to initiating inspection cycles from the secondary inspection list.

3.   If needed, a secondary inspection cycle may be opened before completion of the primary inspection list to:

   a.   Improve the efficiency of the AO, or

   b.   Continue federal agency inspection activity if inspections at some of the primary service/operating locations have been deferred/deleted.

4.   Once any inspection cycle (primary or secondary) is opened, it must be completed.

B.   Personal Security Clearance and Advanced Notice.

1.   Under most circumstances, a CSHO will not need a personal security clearance prior to entering a federal establishment to conduct a FEDTARG inspection. If a federal establishment requires a security clearance, the CSHO should follow the procedure found in the *Field Operations Manual* (FOM), Chapter 3, paragraph II.G., *Personal Security Clearance*.

2.   Given the current National threat level and the unique security needs of some federal departments/agencies, such as the Department of Justice – Bureau of Prisons, a CSHO may be required to obtain a specific personal security clearance(s) for the establishment being inspected. This requirement may necessitate advanced planning by the AO and, in some cases, may delay the opening of the inspection. Advance notice to the establishment may also be required.

   a.   When a CSHO must obtain a specific personal security clearance, the AO should make every effort to maintain the "unannounced" status of the inspection. The AO should request that the establishment's security office not announce the upcoming inspection to the service/operating location.

   b.   The CSHO should follow the establishment's procedures for obtaining a specific personal security clearance.

C.   Inspection Priority.

1. An AO's first inspection priority is to conduct unprogrammed inspections as outlined in CPL 02-00-150, Chapter 2, IV.B., *Inspection Priority Criteria*.

2. An AO will follow the inspection priorities as described in CPL 02-00-150, with the following additional guidance.

   a. Under normal circumstances, incomplete establishment inspections must be completed before beginning a new inspection cycle.

   b. Carryover inspections will be handled in accordance with paragraph B.1.b(1)(e), *Inspection Scheduling,* found in CPL 02-00-025, *Scheduling System for Programmed Inspections*, and as outlined in paragraph XII., *FEDTARG Planning and Scheduling*, in this directive.

3. All establishments on a FEDTARG inspection list must be inspected.

   a. However, an RA may request approval from the Assistant Secretary of Labor for OSHA to delete establishment inspections for a variety of reasons. Examples of such circumstances include, but are not limited to, resource limitations or involvement in National catastrophe/emergency response efforts.

   b. The RA/AD should document the rationale for the deletion in accordance with paragraph XII.E., *FEDTARG Inspection Deletions,* in this directive.

4. Secondary inspection cycles do not have to be completed before the expiration of this directive. However, if an inspection cycle has commenced, all establishments on the inspection list must be inspected prior to initiating establishment inspections under a successive FEDTARG.

5. The goals of the RO/AO will dictate other programmed inspections captured under National Emphasis Program (NEP) or Local Emphasis Program (LEP) initiatives.

D. <u>FEDTARG Inspection Deferrals: Interface with Cooperative Program Participants</u>.

   1. OSHA Strategic Partnership Program for Worker Safety and Health (OSPP). The CSHO should contact the Regional OSPP

Coordinator/Manager with any questions regarding a specific establishment or any of its service/operating locations.

2.   Voluntary Protection Programs (VPP) Applicant.

    a.   If an establishment is in the process of applying for OSHA VPP status, the AD, upon receiving notification from the VPP Manager that a VPP on-site review has been scheduled, will defer the establishment from any programmed inspection.

    b.   If an establishment is a VPP applicant, and a VPP on-site review is scheduled within the next 75 calendar days, programmed inspections will be deferred. Check the VPP website for a current listing of Federal agencies participating in VPP.

    c.   For other VPP site inspection guidance, see CSP 03-01-003.

E.   FEDTARG Inspection Deletions.

1.   Upon approval from the Assistant Secretary of Labor for OSHA, an RA may delete establishment inspections for a variety of reasons, as noted in paragraph XII.C.3.a. of this directive.

2.   The AD is responsible for making appropriate deletions from the inspection list as indicated below.

    a.   Previous Inspections. Only establishments that received a comprehensive safety inspection within the 24 months prior to the creation of the current inspection cycle will be deleted from the inspection list. This timeframe will be calculated using the previous inspection's opening conference date. Note that this does not apply to airport traffic control towers inspected under the FAA AIRTRAF Program.

    b.   Voluntary Protection Programs. If the establishment is an approved VPP participant, it should be deleted from the inspection list in accordance with CSP 03-01-003. Refer to the OSHA VPP website at http://www.osha.gov/dcsp/vpp/index.html, under Participant Information for a current listing of all VPP locations, public and private. Refer to CPL 02-00-150, Chapter 2, for further guidance.

XIII.   FEDTARG Inspections: Relationship to Other Programs.

A. Unprogrammed Inspections. Unprogrammed inspections will be conducted according to CPL 02-00-150 and/or other applicable OSHA policies and procedures. If a need for an unprogrammed inspection arises, such as a complaint or fatality, for an establishment that is also on a current FEDTARG inspection list (primary or secondary), the two inspections may be conducted either concurrently or separately. See also paragraph XVII.B. of this directive.

B. Special Emphasis Program (SEP) Inspections. Some establishments may be selected for inspection under the current FEDTARG and also under other OSHA initiatives, such as a national emphasis program (NEP) or a local emphasis program (LEP). Programs based on particular hazards, such as amputations, combustible dust, etc., or on a particular industry, such as the Nursing industry, petroleum refineries, etc., may be run concurrently with the current FEDTARG. The CSHO should apply all applicable IMIS/OIS codes to the inspection. See paragraph XVII.C. of this directive for further guidance.

C. Inspections Under Both FEDTARG and NEP/LEP. If an establishment is scheduled for inspection under both FEDTARG and an NEP/LEP, the CSHO may conduct an inspection limited in scope to the safety and health issues targeted by the NEP/LEP program. This decision should be based on a review of the OSHA-300 logs and a determination of whether the particular NEP/LEP addresses the serious hazards associated with the establishment. Justification for the limited scope inspection must be documented in the case file.

XIV. FEDTARG Specific Inspection Procedures.

A. Scope. FEDTARG inspections will be comprehensive safety inspections. Health inspections (comprehensive or partial) will be limited to CSHO referrals and AD discretion based on industry experience or the establishment's safety and health history. Ergonomic hazards will be addressed in consultation with the Regional ergonomics coordinator. For inspection guidance for hazards observed outside of the physical location being inspected, see CPL 02-00-150.

B. Use of Alternate, Supplementary Standards. Several federal agencies have alternate and/or supplementary standards. Agencies with alternate standards include:

   • Federal Aviation Administration (FAA), The Alternate Standard for Fire Safety in Airport Traffic Control Towers, May 6, 1998. [intranet page, PDF]
   • National Aeronautics and Space Administration, Standard for Lifting Devices and Equipment, May 9, 2002. [intranet page, PDF]

- U.S. General Services Administration (GSA), Standard on Special-Purpose Ladders Used in Federal Archives and Records Centers, December 9, 1983. [intranet page, PDF]
- U.S. Navy, Naval Facilities Engineering Command Management of Weight Handling Equipment, June 2003. [intranet page, PDF]
- U.S. Navy (USN), Gas Free Engineering Manual.

Agencies with supplementary standards include:

- National Aeronautics and Space Administration (NASA), Safety Standard for Explosives, Propellants and Pyrotechnics, August 1993. [intranet page, PDF]

The CSHO should be familiar with any applicable alternate and/or supplementary standards relevant to the federal establishment being inspected (Current alternate and supplementary standards are provided above.). Refer to the OFAP webpage, http://intranet.osha.gov/compliance/dep_fap.html, for recently approved alternate and supplementary standards added after the effective date of this directive.

In addition, each RO is encouraged to develop Regional SEPs for federal agencies having alternate and/or supplementary standards, such as an SEP based on any of the FAA, GSA, NASA, or USN alternate and supplementary standards. These SEPs will not be limited to the provisions of the respective Federal agency's alternate or supplementary standard. Rather, these SEPs will be conducted as comprehensive safety inspections.

C. FEDTARG Health Inspection. When an AD orders a health inspection (comprehensive or partial) of an establishment, the AD must document the rationale for the inspection in accordance with paragraph XVI. *Case File Documentation*, in this directive.

1. If an AD authorizes a health inspection of an establishment based on experience or industry knowledge, similar health inspections must also be considered at all other establishments within that industry classification that are on the AO's FEDTARG inspection list (primary or secondary).

2. The AD has the discretion to initiate a health inspection based solely on individual establishment criteria or history.

3. Inspections will be conducted in accordance with the procedures described in CPL 02-00-150 and other guidance documents.

D. Federal Agencies with Private Sector Employees On-site.

1.	At service/operating locations where the CSHO observes contractors performing other work, such as construction or maintenance activity that is not being supervised by the site's federal agency personnel, the CSHO may open another inspection if he/she observes hazards, or if the activity is consistent with any NEP or LEP currently in effect. The inspection will be expanded to include resident contractors providing services, such as security, food service, or housekeeping only when the CSHO observes obvious hazards that need to be addressed. Refer to Chapter 3, paragraph VII.J., *Multi-employer worksites,* in CPL 02-00-150, for further guidance.

2.	State Plan Jurisdiction on Federal Property. Refer to CPL 02-00-150, Chapter 13, II.D.a., for further guidance on state program jurisdiction on federal property. Coverage is set out in various documents including operational status agreements and final approval decisions which are codified at 29 CFR Part 1952. The RA must refer to the appropriate State, subject to 29 CFR Part 1952, and supporting documents to determine jurisdiction.

3.	The CSHO should refer to CPL 02-00-150, Chapter 13, II.D., for guidance regarding Government-Owned Contractor-Operated Facilities (GOCOs), Department of Energy sites, and private sector employees and other agencies' jurisdictions.

E.	Partnership Sites. An inspection at any partnership site will normally be a comprehensive safety inspection. However, if the establishment has undergone a necessary on-site non-enforcement verification inspection, a limited scope inspection may be conducted in accordance with paragraph XIV.B.4. in CSP 03-02-002. Also see paragraph XII.C., *FEDTARG Inspection Deferrals: Interface with Cooperative Program Participants*, in this directive for further guidance. The justification for any limited scope inspection must be documented in the case file.

F.	Establishments with Multiple Services/Operations. A federal establishment may provide multiple services/operations at a single physical location. For example, a Federal Correctional Complex (FCC) may include multiple Bureau of Prisons establishments within the single complex. These service/operating locations may include a high security prison facility with other lower security facilities [such as a single or multiple UNICOR facility(ies)].

A federal establishment may also perform activities outside of the physical location being inspected. These activities may be governed by written occupational safety and health protocols. For example, the United States Department of Agriculture – Forest Service performs trail clearing activities in forested areas under their jurisdiction. Likewise, the Department of the Interior - Bureau of Land Management performs logging operations in areas under their jurisdiction. In such cases, the CSHO may consider opening an inspection for activities under the establishment's jurisdiction but performed outside of the physical location being inspected under a FEDTARG inspection cycle. The CSHO should review and analyze these programs for possible inspection activity. The CSHO must be aware of RO/ AO jurisdictional boundaries; a referral inspection may be necessary.

1. When a CSHO arrives at an establishment and observes multiple services/operations present at the single physical location, the CSHO will review the OSHA 300 log(s) or the agency's equivalent injury and illness log(s) from the previous year(s) to identify the establishment's services/operating locations with higher LTCs.

2. The CSHO will consult with the AD. The AD will determine the appropriate number and location of on-site inspections necessary to adequately address the safety and health issues present at the establishment, but at least one (1) service/operating location must be inspected.

3. If the AD determines that more than one (1) service/operating location needs to be inspected, the service/operating locations may be randomly chosen or the decision may be based on the service/operating locations experiencing the highest number of LTCs. For each distinct service/operating location selected, the CSHO will open a separate FEDTARG inspection.

G. Office Only Operating Locations. The intent of FEDTARG to focus on establishment service/operating locations having high LTCs, not on establishments that are solely office environments. However, if the office environment is experiencing a high number of LTCs, the office service/operating location will be inspected.

1. If a CSHO arrives at an establishment that is solely an office environment, has reason to believe that the establishment is the "clearinghouse" for OWCP reporting purposes, or the establishment address does not reflect the location where LTCs are occurring, the CSHO must determine if other service/operating locations were included as part of the OWCP identified "establishment." For example, a human resources office may be identified with a large number of LTCs when in actuality the LTCs are associated with smaller but potentially more hazardous establishment service/operating locations.

16

2.   In the preceding situation, the CSHO will review the injury and illness logs to identify a limited number of the establishment's service/operating locations with the highest LTCs. The CSHO will consult with the AD.

3.   The AD will determine the appropriate number and location of on-site inspections necessary to adequately address the safety and health issues present in the establishment, but at least one service/operating location must be inspected. If the AD determines that more than one (1) service/operating location needs to be inspected, the service/operating locations may be randomly chosen, or the decision may be based on the service/operating locations experiencing the highest number of LTCs. For each distinct service/operating location selected, the CSHO will open a separate FEDTARG inspection.

H.   Safety and Health FEDTARG Inspections.

1.   When the AD has authorized a health inspection in conjunction with a FEDTARG safety inspection, the safety and health inspections may be conducted as:

a.   One combined safety and health inspection by a cross-trained CSHO (as established through specific training or demonstrated ability), or

b.   Separate safety and health inspections, or

c.   Joint safety and health inspections.

2.   Documentation for Safety and Health Inspection.

a.   OSHA 1. When a joint safety and health inspection is conducted by a safety CSHO and a health CSHO, each CSHO will complete an appropriate OSHA 1 in accordance with CPL 02-00-150, Chapter 5, *Case File Preparation and Documentation*. The safety CSHO will complete an OSHA 1 for the safety inspection; the health CSHO will complete an OSHA 1 for the health inspection. Therefore, there will be two (2) OSHA 1 forms for the same establishment inspection under the same FEDTARG inspection.

b.   Opening Conference. The two (2) CSHOs assigned to the joint safety and health inspection may hold joint or separate opening conferences. Therefore, there may be one (1) opening date for the

17

safety inspection and a different opening date for the health inspection for the same establishment under the same FEDTARG inspection.

c.   Safety and Health Inspections. If a CSHO is qualified to conduct both a safety inspection and the health inspection, the CSHO needs only to complete one (1) OSHA-1 form with one (1) opening conference date annotated.

XV.   Violations.

A.   Notice of Unsafe or Unhealthful Working Conditions OSHA-2H Form (OSHA Notice). Notices to federal establishments will be issued as required by 29 CFR 1960.31(d), and in accordance with 29 CFR 1960.26(c) and CPL 02-00-150, Chapter 4, *Violations*.

1.   The general duty requirements for federal agencies are referenced in 29 CFR 1960.8, *Agency responsibilities*.

2.   Under FEDTARG, an OSHA Notice may be issued for violations of an agency's alternate standard and/or supplementary standard. In these cases, the OSHA Notice will be developed and issued in accordance with CPL 02-00-150, *Field Operations Manual*, and FAP 01-00-003 *Federal Agency Safety and Health Programs,* paragraph L. 1: *Issuance of the OSHA Notice*. The federal agency adjustments will be followed when issuing the OSHA Notice for violations of an agency's alternate and/or supplementary standards.

a.   For violations of an alternate standard where requirements are also addressed in OSHA standards, the CSHO should: (a) cite the OSHA standard; (b) enter "As required by 29 CFR 1960.8(b)" in the SAVEs standard language section; and (c) reference the unmet provision of the alternate standard in the Alleged Violation Description.

b.   For violations of a provision of an alternate standard that are not a requirement in 29 CFR 1910, the CSHO should cite 29 CFR 1960.8(a), and reference the violated paragraph of the alternate standard.

c.   For violations of a requirement in 29 CFR 1910 that are not addressed in an alternate standard, the CSHO should cite the violated OSHA standard, and enter "As required by 29 CFR 1960.8(b)" to the SAVEs standard language section.

    d.   For violations of a provision of a supplementary standard, the CSHO should cite 29 CFR 1960.8(a) and reference the violated paragraph of the supplementary standard.

B.   <u>Recordkeeping Violations</u>. Whenever a CSHO identifies an OSHA recordkeeping violation, the CSHO will propose the appropriate notices and provide supporting documentation, in accordance with the policies and procedures found in CPL 02-00-135; CPL 02-00-150, Chapter 3, VI.C., *Recordkeeping Deficiencies*, or successors.

C.   <u>Violations Regarding Access to Medical Records</u>. Whenever a CSHO identifies violations of employer compliance with medical recordkeeping requirements, the CSHO will propose the appropriate notices and provide supporting documentation, in accordance with the policies and procedures found in CPL 02-02-072, Chapter XV, *Citation Guidelines.*

D.   <u>FEDTARG Compliance Safety and Health Officer Checklist</u>. The CSHO should refer to Appendix A of this directive for items they need to accomplish during FEDTARG inspections.

XVI.   <u>Case File Documentation</u>.

A.   The AD is responsible for maintaining case file documentation to demonstrate that the FEDTARG inspection lists (primary and secondary) have been used in accordance with the requirements of this directive. Documentation should include a rationale for all deletions, deferrals, or other modifications to the original inspection lists, such as a reason for expanding specific inspection(s) to cover health hazards, based on either experience or industry knowledge.

B.   In accordance with CPL 02-00-025, paragraph B.1.b.(1)(c)3., the AO must maintain all inspection lists, cycles, and documentation for a period of three (3) years after completing all inspections conducted under the current FEDTARG directive. ADM 03-01-005, Appendix D, *Compliance Records Disposition Schedule,* should be consulted for an acceptable disposition schedule.

XVII.   <u>Recording and Tracking</u>.

A.   <u>FEDTARG12-Only Inspections</u>. The OSHA-1 form must be marked as "programmed planned" in *Item 24*. In addition, the *"NEP"* box is to be checked and the value "FEDTARG12" recorded in *Item 25d.*

NOTE 1:   The FEDTARG12 inspections are being coded under the NEP for ease of tracking.

NOTE 2:   Health inspections conducted in accordance with this directive are to be coded as "FEDTARG12" inspections.

B.   FEDTARG12-Combined with Unprogrammed Inspections. For all unprogrammed inspections conducted in conjunction with a FEDTARG12 inspection, the OSHA-1 form must be marked as "unprogrammed" in *Item 24* with the appropriate unprogrammed activity identified. In addition, the *"NEP"* box is to be checked and the value "FEDTARG12" recorded in *Item 25d*.

C.   FEDTARG12-Combined with NEP or LEP Inspections. For all programmed inspections, such as NEPs and LEPs, conducted in conjunction with a FEDTARG 12 inspection, the OSHA-1 form must be marked as "programmed planned" in *Item 24*. In addition, the *"NEP"* box is to be checked and the value "FEDTARG 12" recorded in *Item 25d* along with all NEP and LEP IMIS/ OIS codes applicable to the inspection.

D.   FEDTARG12-Combined with Unprogrammed and Other Programmed Inspections. If a FEDTARG12 inspection is combined with an unprogrammed inspection, such as an inspection generated through a complaint, and a programmed inspection, such as a NEP or LEP, then *Item 24* must be marked "unprogrammed."

E.   OSHA Strategic Management Plan. Enter all applicable OSHA Strategic Management Plan hazard/industry codes in *Item 25f*. Some examples of entries may include, but are not limited to, amputations, ergonomics, lead, silica.

APPENDIX A

Federal Agency Targeting Inspection Program

Compliance Safety and Health Officer Checklist

I. Voluntary Protection Programs (VPP) Sites

    A. If the CSHO discovers that the establishment is a Voluntary Protection Programs (VPP) Merit or Star site, the CSHO should exit the site without conducting an inspection. These sites must be deleted from the inspection list. See CPL 02-00-150, and paragraph XII.E.2. of this directive for further guidance.

    B. If an establishment is a VPP applicant, and a VPP on-site review is scheduled within the next 75 calendar days, programmed inspections will be deferred. See paragraph XII.D.2. of this directive.

II. Integrated Management Information System (IMIS)

    A. Enter Agency Code

        Use the "F7" search feature to locate the appropriate code[1].

    B. Enter Inspection Classification

        Inspection classification: NEP = "FEDTARG12"

    C. Enter all applicable NEP/LEP program codes

        In *Item(s) 25c* and *25d* when a federal agency targeting inspection was conducted and the inspection also meets the protocol for other program(s).

    D. Enter all applicable OSHA Strategic Management Plan hazard/industry codes

        In *Item 25f* (such as, amputations, ergonomics, lead and silica).

---

1 The newly established OSHA Information System (OIS) uses drop down menus to locate codes; therefore, the functions keys may be inoperable if entering into the OIS.)

E.   <u>Enter Inspection Type</u>

For:	Enter:
FEDTARG12-Only Inspections	Programmed Planned
FEDTARG12-Combined with Unprogrammed Inspections	Unprogrammed
FEDTARG12-Combined with LEP Inspections	Programmed Planned
FEDTARG12-Combined with Unprogrammed and Other Programmed	Unprogrammed

APPENDIX B

Federal Agency Targeting Inspection Program

Abbreviations, Acronyms and Symbol used in this directive

AD	Area Director
ADM	Directorate of Administrative Programs directive
AIRTRAF	FAA Airport Traffic Control Tower Monitoring Program
AO	Area Office
CFR	Code of Federal Regulations
CPL	Directorate of Enforcement Programs directive
CSHC	Certified Safety and Health Committee
CSHO	Compliance Safety and Health Officer
CSP	Directorate of Cooperative and State Programs directive
DEP	Directorate of Enforcement Programs
DOL	U.S. Department of Labor
FAA	Federal Aviation Administration
FAP	Office of Federal Agency Programs directive
FAPO	Federal Agency Program Officer
FEDTARG12	Federal Agency Targeting Inspection Program 2012
FOM	Field Operations Manual
FR	Federal Register
FY	Fiscal Year
GOCO	Government-Owned Contractor-Operated
GSA	U.S. General Services Administration
IMIS	Integrated Management Information System
LEP	Local Emphasis Program
LTC	Lost time case
NASA	National Aeronautics and Space Administration
NEP	National Emphasis Program
NO	National Office
OFAP	Office of Federal Agency Programs
OIS	OSHA Information System
OSHA	Occupational Safety and Health Administration
OSPP	OSHA Strategic Partnership Program
OWCP	Department of Labor - Office of Workers' Compensation Programs
RA	Regional Administrator
RO	Regional Office
SEP	Special Emphasis Program
USN	U.S. Navy
VPP	Voluntary Protection Programs
§	Section symbol (signum sectionis)

www.ingramcontent.com/pod-product-compliance
Lightning Source LLC
Chambersburg PA
CBHW082305200526
45168CB00018B/3421